Marriage Is Honorable

Felisa M. Burnside

WestBow
PRESS
A DIVISION OF THOMAS NELSON

WestBow Press books may be ordered through booksellers or by contacting:

WestBow Press
A Division of Thomas Nelson
1663 Liberty Drive
Bloomington, IN 47403
www.westbowpress.com
1-(866) 928-1240

Because of the dynamic nature of the Internet, any web addresses or
links contained in this book may have changed since publication and
may no longer be valid. The views expressed in this work are solely those
of the author and do not necessarily reflect the views of the publisher,
and the publisher hereby disclaims any responsibility for them.

Any people depicted in stock imagery provided by Thinkstock are models,
and such images are being used for illustrative purposes only.

Certain stock imagery © Thinkstock.

ISBN: 978-1-4497-1582-3 (sc)

Library of Congress Control Number: 2011927027

Printed in the United States of America

WestBow Press rev. date: 05/05/2011

Intro
This Is From A Child's Point Of View.

What I can first recollect about marriage was when I was five years old. My dad and mom had recently gone through a divorce. The only thing I understood about this was that my dad did not live at home anymore. My dad picked me up one afternoon for my routine ride after school. He had this thing about getting me alone and telling me what he wanted me to believe. He proceeded to tell me how my mom had put him out of the house and he was living in his car. This hurt me so deeply and I remember crying and becoming very upset with my mom. When I arrived home I began to tell my mom what I had heard.

My mom sat me down and begins to tell me how my dad lived in the same neighborhood, around the corner with another woman and her daughter. At first I thought, "What a lie, this couldn't be". I don't know what prompted her to do what she did next, but she put me in the car and drove me two blocks and showed me where his car was parked. This was the most heartbreaking day of my little life.

I then spent most of my adolescent and teenage years trying to figure out how this happened. Although I was very young I understood how things were suppose to be. Dad was supposed to be coming home to us but he wasn't. As a teenager, I found myself thrust in the middle of many heated disputes. It was hard for me to understand what part I played in all of this. My dad was a busy man. He was a school teacher by day and was the lead singer in a band by night. My mom was a homemaker caring for me, my older brother and two younger siblings. We belonged to the local Baptist Church where my great-grandmother attended. My dad also played the bass guitar and sang with the choir. From the outside looking in, we may have looked like the ideal family. But we were actually the definition of, "looks are deceiving".

My dad accused my mom of cheating. However, he failed to mention that he came into the marriage with four daughters the same age. Yes, I did say the same age. He married my mom and five more children were born. Two children died at birth. As an adult, to put all of this into perspective, my dad had a lot of explaining to do. I spent most of my adult years being angry with my dad because he was a liar. He ended up with 12 children with seven mamas. I promise you I was full grown and in my thirties before I could put all this drama together. But nevertheless, I suffered greatly behind their decision to be divorced. I realize now that sometimes there is nothing you can do to save a marriage. Sometimes, you have to move on. Situations like these must be handled decently and orderly. There is no excuse for making the children suffer. I feel that the children are the top priority when considering the dissolution of marriage.

As a child of divorce, I suffered physically, financially and spiritually. I was thrust into a cruel world without a foundation to stand on. My future was dim and I could see no way out. But God! Who is rich in mercy, gave me a sound mind and a determination to triumph. I now see how God's love and protection covered me and kept me. I made up my mind at around 15-years old, that my life would not be a disaster. I knew I needed God in my life. Even though I didn't know God as my personal savior, I knew him and his power to change people and give them a mind to change their situation. My goals in life were, God, a husband, a home and definitely children. I made a vow to myself that my marriage would be my top priority. It would be the one thing that would directly affect how I viewed success in my world. And believe me; my world wasn't very big at this point. Marriage was the one thing I needed to know could work. I knew that it would take great faith on my part to make it work. Little did I know I would not have everything under control in my own world? God is the builder of a good marriage. You will have issues and problems. You can work through them with an open mind and good communication. If you want it, you can do it. If there is a will, there is a way.

Marriage will not always be roses and candy kisses. Sometimes it gets heated down to where the rubber meets the road and a blow out is inevitable. But God! Who is rich in mercy allows U-turns. He allows self examination and round table discussions. I can remember the early years of my marriage when William and I would become angry with one another and be in the same house for days and not even speak to each other. This was a foolish choice, but no matter what the situation was, divorce was never an option. We've always known we loved each other. We were very immature early in our marriage and did not make wise choices at times.

It was obvious that we had no blue print to follow. We had similar goals and with lots of love we built a strong foundation. As we have matured and grew wiser in the word of God, we now realize that being angry and going to bed is not of God.

Ephesians 4:26, 27. 26(KJV) "Be ye angry, and sin not: let not the sun go down upon your wrath: 27-Neither give place to the devil."

The most sure things I know about marriage is that it must be done God's way. Marriage will have to be on God's terms. Marriage is a process of good and bad, high and low. If you cannot go through the process of trials and tests you will never reap the rewards God has for your marriage. Be blessed in the simple things that God has given me to share with you. Keep an open mind, be willing to compromise and give unselfishly to your mate and you will see the great benefits in working to have a happy marriage.

Love

1st Corinthians 13:4-8. (KJV) "Love is patient, love is kind. It does not envy, it does not boast, it is not proud. Love is not rude, it is not self-seeking, it is not easily angered, and it keeps no record of wrongs. Love does not delight in evil, but rejoices with the truth. Loves bears all things, believes all things hopes for all things, endures all things. Love never fails."

"It was Love that made atonement for all of our sins on the cross. Love was oppressed and afflicted, yet he opened not his mouth. Love was brought as a lamb to the slaughter and as a sheep before shearers and Love opened not his mouth." Isaiah 54:7(KJV) The very next time you think that you are going through a hard time in your marriage, a time when you feel like you just cannot go on, think on these things about Love. Love made the greatest sacrifice and that is what true love is all about. St John 5:12-13(KJV) "This is my commandment that you love one another, as I have loved you. Greater love hath no man than this that a man lay down his life for his friends." The example that we should follow is God's love for his people. In a marriage, we are inclined to think only of Romantic love. Romantic love does have its place in a marriage. However, if we do not learn to love unconditionally, we miss the whole point.

God's love for us is unconditional. Love is not what you feel, it's what you do. Feelings, emotions and hormones change to frequently to be called love. The love God has for his church can only be compared to one other love. That is the love that Christ commanded a man to have for his wife. These two loves must be unconditional. The covenant love a man has for his wife must be rooted in Jesus. If a man will not seek the Lord to fulfill the love bank of his wife then he may run the risk of having a bankrupt marriage. Some men are never taught to love as boys and in turn, it is reflected in the lack of love he has for the woman he marries. He may feel like, "I'm paying the bills and taking care of the kids and that's love." I'm not referring to that type of contaminated love. That type of love is obligated love. I'm talking about the unadulterated love that God commanded a man to have for his wife.

The thing that makes this love so unique is that a man has to seek God to find out how to do this. Many men will not take the time to search the scriptures and apply them to daily living. So they miss the mark so far off in loving the one person God commanded them to love.

For all the wives trying to figure out how to fall deeper in love with your husband, there is no such thing commanded unto you. God has put a special place in a man's heart reserved only for him. God commanded man to" love his wife as Christ loved to church and gave his life for it." Ephesians 5:25. (KJV) When a man accepts and understands what God's agape love is, he can't lose loving his wife.

God never commanded a woman to love a man. Her command is to reverence (respect) him. My husband takes care to leave no stone unturned in our marriage when it comes to loving me. When all the bases are covered, he hits a homerun every time. It is a man's responsibility to teach his wife how to love him. The only reason he will not, is he doesn't know how. If a man will seek God for guidance and revelation, he cannot go wrong. Sure, a man obtains favor from God when he finds a wife. But he will never walk in continual victory until he learns to love her unconditionally as God has commanded.

1st John 4:18 (KJV) "There is no fear in love; but perfect love casts out fear: because fear hath torment. He that fears is not made perfect in love." The average woman is not going to run from a man that loves her completely and unconditionally. If she is made to feel secure and protected, she will make sure he has everything he needs. Affection is a part of that love a man has for his wife. It does not necessarily involve sex. Love is action, but not just in the bedroom. Loving and cherishing the wife should be shown through affection. Physical love will most definitely flourish out of unconditional love. True love is an action, shows up every day and accomplishes what it is suppose to do. True love stays on course and finishes the race.

You can tell a lot about the character of a man in how he treats his wife. God left the wife in the hands and direct authority of the husband. God expects man to treat her like the example he left in his word. Nurture her, pray for her and leave no room for doubt in her mind that you love her. Show up every day and participate in the marriage. Go out of your way for her more than you do for others. Keep your promises to her. Be faithful to her in word and deed. Spend scheduled quality time with her. Talk about her often in your daily journey. Be honest with her. She represents you and how you treat her will show in her demeanor to others and ultimately flow to your children. Love is a powerful emotion. Love envelops the two as one. Love is something that is hard to fall out of. When we drift away from God, he is always tugging at our hearts to come back. He never stops loving us. So it is with a man that loves a woman, he never can see himself without her.

"Love is not an affectionate feeling, but a steady wish for the loved person's ultimate good as far as it can be obtained." (C.S. Lewis)

"You ought to trust me for I do not love and will never love any woman in the world but you, and my chief desire is to link myself to you week by week by bonds which shall ever become more intimate and profound. Beloved I kiss your memory-your sweetness and beauty have cast a glory upon my life." (Sir Winston Churchill, to his wife Clementine) Wow! What a Love. Should we all learn to love this way?

Communication

Communication is the key for the survival of any relationship. If you do not talk to each other, the lines are disconnected. Love cannot flow through disconnected lines.

Your mate will never have a fair chance to love you the way you desire to be loved if you do not communicate those needs to them. Your desires will never be fulfilled if you do not open your mouth and speak those things you desire often. If your mate brings you chocolate on a regular basis and you really like cherry, you have poor lines of communication. Your mate deserves to know what it takes to please you. Communicating needs is a positive part of every relationship. You must open up your mouth and make your needs known in order for love to be reciprocated in a way that is conducive for love and affection.

Communication is the heartbeat of every marriage relationship. If you want to see how long a relationship will last, check its vital signs. It is a sad situation when you hear someone in a marriage say, "we do not talk". Silence is deadly and can kill a marriage faster than adultery. Silence is a poison that taints the roots of a marriage. Silence speaks volumes in a relationship. If you are not talking, you open the door for assumptions. I can just make up what you are saying with your facial expressions and body language. You pass each other in the kitchen and one of you turns side ways to keep from touching the other, deadly! One of you asks a question and the other rolls their eyes to the ceiling and smirks, deadly!

Have you ever been there? Well, don't go there because it is deadly. Take my word for it. It wastes so much time and energy to act foolishly.

1st Corinthians 13:11(KJV) "When I was a child, I spake as child, I understood as a child, I thought as a child: but when I became a man, I put away childish things."

Proverbs 17:28(KJV) "Even a fool, when he holdeth his peace, is counted wise: and he that shutteth his lips is esteemed a man of understanding."

Have you ever watched children play? They play together all day, sometimes they fight over toys and come to adults to referee the fight. Watch those same children at the end of the day and they are playing like nothing ever happened. These children may even hug and kiss before they leave each other and anticipate getting together for the next play date. The moral of this is that communication is clear with these children. We may disagree for a moment, but you should not ever allow disagreement to keep us from communicating effectively about issues that concern our relationship.

I have a serious problem with someone who can go to work all day and greet everyone in the office in a courteous manner and return home like a sour puss. You might say, "That is different, that is my job". No honey, your job is to please your mate, and that means showing up every day and participating in what you signed up for. Your mate deserves a "good morning honey, how did you sleep?" At the end of a long day, they also deserve a "Baby how was your day?" I think everyone of us in a marriage signed up for companionship, friendship and love. If you have come to the point of silence, GET SOME HELP!!

1st Peter 3:7, 8 &9. (KJV) (7) Likewise, ye husbands dwell with them according to knowledge, giving honor unto the wife, as unto the weaker vessel, and as being heirs together of the grace of life; that your prayers be not hindered.

(8) Finally, be ye all of one mind, having compassion one of another, love as brethren, be pitiful, be courteous.

(9) Not rendering evil for evil, or railing for railing: but contra wise blessing; knowing that ye are thereunto called, that ye should inherit a blessing.

Proverbs 31:26 (KJV) "She opened her mouth with wisdom and in her tongue is the law of kindness."

Words are powerful and can have a profound effect on a person. You can either speak life or death into your life or the life of your mate. In turn, you actually affect your own future because whether or not your mate is blessed or cursed, it directly affects you and your own family.

Proverbs 18:21 (KJV) "Death and life are in the power of the tongue: and they that love it shall eat the fruit thereof."

Listening

Listening is also a form of communication. Listening is an art that very few master. Most people have their mind set on preparing what they have to say while another is yet speaking.

However, very few realize that if you never master listening, communication is not complete.

James 1: 19 (KJV) "Wherefore, my beloved brethren, let every man be swift to hear, slow to speak, slow to wrath. "

Listening takes great skill and consideration. It is so hard to sit there and give your full attention to another person without thinking about how you will respond to what they have said. Notice I said, "What they have said", not what you heard them say. Chances are you have only heard only 50% of what they said and the other 50% is assumption. Assumption is a crucial breakdown in any conversation. That is why most experts agree that paraphrasing what you think you just heard is a good idea. This gives the other person a fair chance to clarify exactly what they said. If you listen sharply and think before you speak, communication will go much smoother. Communication is truly a priority in a marriage. There are so many issues that must be discussed.

So many couples encounter surprises later in the marriage because talking was not a priority in the beginning. In the early stages of a relationship when emotions are running high and infatuation and lust may be a factor influencing this romance, many fail to see the signs of miscommunication. Most of us are so busy trying to be socially correct, we forget that this person came from a whole other background than ourselves. This person grew up under different pressures and is driven by totally different motives. We forget to ask what the motives and expectations of the other person is.

William and I never had a problem identifying who we were and what we expected of each other in the marriage. He had found his wife and I had accepted him as a husband. Many couples fail to realize that both of these titles come with totally different roles. If I have said it once, I will say again that God has had a plan for marriage since the beginning of creation.

Genesis 2: 18 (KJV) "And God said, it is not good that the man should be alone; I will make him an help meet for him".

Genesis 2: 21- (21) And the Lord God caused a deep sleep to fall upon Adam, and he slept: and he took one of his ribs, and closed up the flesh instead thereof;

(22)- And the rib, which the Lord God had taken from man, made him a woman, and brought her unto a man.

Seeking Her

God had a perfect plan before the fall of man in the Garden of Eden. If it is not your desire to seek his plan in his word for your marriage, you will need to have the faith to believe that marriage between a man and a woman was ordained by God in the beginning. After Adam received his wife from God, God gave every man after Adam a command, "leave father and mother and take care of your wife." The wife is supposed to be the closest being to that husband. God's plan has great benefits for the man that seeks a wife.

Proverbs 18:22 (KJV) "Whoso findeth a wife findeth a good thing, and obtaineth favor of the Lord."

Favor- prefers, like, approve of, praise, regard favorably, choose, and lean toward, value and think well of.

(Laird, C.Websters New World Thesaurus. 3rd Ed. 2003. Wiley Publishing. Cleveland Ohio.).

Adam was the only man that God chose a wife for. God's specifications were applicable for Adam's wife. Adam had the favor of God on him at the very beginning of creation. God created Adam in his image and made his wife from a part of him. She was taken from man and called woman. God's perfect plan included man having a helpmate. From that day forward, every man after Adam must seek her. He must first seek God and ask God for his specific mate. When God approves a man's choice, he obtains favor of the Lord. This says to me that God believes in specification. A man should not have to go out taste testing and saying "I love you and want you to be my wife" to any average female. She must be specifically for you, for your personality, for you character and for your plans. Your personality and Godliness will draw her, your character will keep her and your plans for her must sell her. The rib was chosen as a specific part of God's plan. Ribs are anatomically and strategically placed where they are for a special reason. Ribs surround the heart and protect it. Ribs allow expansion of the respiratory system and other vital organs. Ribs are attached to the spine (backbone). The head is at the end of the rib closest to the vertebral column. The sternum is the breast plate that connects the true ribs. It is important to have the right rib relationship. The wrong rib connection can be detrimental for life. One key point to remember is that broken ribs hurt in the natural and spiritual realm. Men, please protect your rib because your rib is what God gave to protect you. When God presents Adam his bride, Adam makes the most profound statement ever. All men should take notice and keep this tradition going.

Genesis 2:23-24 (KJV) And Adam said this is now bone of my bones, and flesh of my flesh: she shall be called Woman, because she was taken out of Man. Therefore shall a man leave his father and mother and shall cleave unto his wife: and they shall be one flesh.

There is a treasure waiting for every man that seeks God for his wife. A man is a hunter by nature and should be allowed a chance to pursue his mate. Women should not be out looking for him, but making herself ready for his coming. Remember when God said he was coming back for a church that had made herself ready? God said "without spot or blemish or any such thing." The church should be getting ready every day for the coming of Christ. In the same manner, a woman should be making herself ready for her husband. Presentation is a priority to a man. My husband always says when he gets his meal placed on the table in front of him that he eats with his eyes first. How a woman presents herself in public, in church and on her job screams specifications. According to the world, a man is looking for his dime piece, his perfect "10". That is what he recognizes when he finds it. In marriage, you can't "fake it until you make it".

My husband says that a woman will say she is looking for a genuine man. But, when he finds her, she is wearing a wig or weaves, press on lashes, and make up, girdles and three inch heels. She wants a real man when everything about her is deceptive. Women need to be real when they are waiting on their husbands "Realistic" would be the right word to use. Chances are your husband is not going to look like Denzel Washington or Brad Pitt. Choose your battles wisely ladies or you will wait forever until Jesus comes and then you can be his bride. When your husband finds you, you must be the ready rib that he's looking for. You cannot be so specific about what you want and not bring anything to the table. Are you waiting for good looks or Godly character? If you answered both, you might get lucky, but chances are God has just the right package for you. That package could possibly include both. Just in case it doesn't, keep your spiritual ear tuned and God will deliver the right package tailor made just for you.

Favored by God

Proverbs 18:22 (KJV) "Whoso findeth a wife, findeth a good thing and obtaineth favor of the Lord."

There is no better place to be after being saved by the blood of Jesus, than to be favored by God. If you have chosen to follow the Lord, would you not want to be in his favor? A man favored by God can avoid so many pitfalls along the way. You will indeed encounter issues, challenges and other distractions along this walk with God. But none of these are too hard for God to handle.

In this case, you must not only be willing to follow God, but you must also be willing to stand in the gap for your marriage and family. This will require dedicated time in the presence of God through what we know as prayer. You must take time to establish and nurture a relationship with him to be favored by him. Trusting God with your marriage will take great effort on your part. Since the enemy knows that God models marriage after his relationship with his church, he has been doing everything within his power to destroy marriage. Satan succeeded in the destruction of Adam and Eves Union, and men and women have been falling for the same trick ever since. Satan has followed the same plan since the garden and it's now called "No fault or Irreconcilable". Does either one of those sound familiar to you? If so, you may know someone who has been deceived by one of them. The world dresses them up and hopes you will be enticed to make a move for the grass that looks greener on the other side.

Sadly, many don't survive the journey to the other side and cannot tell of its goodness. They tend to discover shortly after they arrive to the other side that it is only artificial turf. What you set out to accomplish in one marriage will have to be done the same way in the next marriage. Again I say, if it is not done God's way, there will not be any way it can be done. You have to become a visionary for your marriage. You have to see the good in your mate and cultivate it. You must water it with love and affection, time and commitment and watch what God can grow out of these seeds that you invest into your mate. Sure you can pluck away at their faults and surly they will be magnified. But when you start looking through the eyes of God you can see greatness start to evolve. God wants to give you great. Allow him. You will be surprised what can happen with God and time

God's Model For Marriage

Ephesians 5:21-33(KJV)

21-Submitting yourselves one to another in the fear of God. 22-Wives submit yourselves unto your own husbands, as unto the Lord. 23- For the husband is the head of the wife, even as Christ is the head of the church: and he is the savior of the body. 24- Therefore as the Church is subject unto Church, so let the wives be to their own husbands in everything. 25- Husbands, love your wives, even as Christ also loved the church, and gave himself for it: 26- That he might sanctify and cleanse it with the washing of water by the word. 27- That he might present it to himself it to himself a glorious church, not having spot, or wrinkle, or any such thing; but that it should be holy and without blemish. 28- So ought men to love their wives as their own bodies. He that loveth his wife loveth himself. 29- For no man ever yet hated his own flesh; but nourisheth and cherisheth it, even as the Lord the church: 30- For we are members of his body, of his flesh, and his bones. 31-For this cause shall a man leave his father and mother, and shall be joined unto his wife, and they two shall be one flesh. 32-This is a great mystery but I speak concerning Christ and the church.

33- Nevertheless let every one of you in particular so love his wife even as himself; and the wife that she reverence her husband.

If it were pleasing to my God, I would close the book and tell you to do what you just read, but understanding is the key to being able to obey the word of God. Comprehending the word of God will take revelation from the Holy Ghost. The Holy Ghost will guide you into all truth and reveal those things that appear foreign to you. I feel the scriptures in Ephesians will make for a good marriage book club reading with discussions. There are many different beliefs about what people think would make marriage work. Great psychologists have developed five-step plans to save your marriage and habits of a happy home. There is not a step, plan or habit developed by man that could secure a marriage in this day and age. We are living in a day of deception. TV, internet and magazines have developed this image of a fine young blonde or brown skinned woman who is curvaceous and sexy. And men around the world have decided that this is the ideal mate. She can't cook, take care of a home or you, but this image is unforgettable in your mind. The impression this image will leave on your mind is inescapable. You will find yourself drifting further and further away from the plan that God has for your marriage.

The same scenario goes for the woman who desires a husband. You have this image of your knight in shining armor riding up in a Benz with his pockets laced with money ready to take you on a trip around the world. What if he's the janitor in your building or at the church, the one with the tooth missing on the side, barely making ends meet? Well, I guess I may have gone to the extreme with that one, but he may not be a GQ model. He just may be your average guy. But if God wants to give you a great guy in the average man and you are blinded by the cares of what the world expects for you, you will never be able to see a future in that. For one thing, a woman needs to be praying for a husband and God will supply one when she is mentally and spiritually mature enough to handle one. And the man should be seeking God for his wife since God will return favor when he finds her. Someone once said that "a woman's' heart should be so deeply rooted in God that a man will have to seek God to find her." I really like that quote. If women would take heed to it and bury their heart in God's word, it would save a lot of heartache and pain. Many men like only what they see and when they lay two or three lame lines down to the woman, buy a chicken dinner and text her four times, she is in love. How simple can one continue to be? He didn't pray about it, look for it or ask for it, you just give it so freely. Women, we need to learn how to be women of God.

Married women, testify to your unwed sisters in Christ. Plead with them to wait on God for a husband. It is not an easy task when they see women enjoying their husbands. But those who have not yet married will never begin to understand the work it takes to keep a marriage together. Ok, back to the issue at hand, God's model for marriage.

Ephesians 5:21-33(KJV)

21- Submitting yourselves to one another in the fear of God. Submit means to give into or surrender to another's authority. Pleasing your mate should be your only agenda. Taking care of their needs and allowing yourself to be a servant to them. If you serve each other, no one's needs are left unmet. Put your mate first; don't plan a night out with the girls or boys without making sure the needs at home are met. But know and understand that God will be pleased that you took care of the mate he blessed you with. This is your blessing to God, that you submit yourself to one another.

22-Wives, submit yourselves unto your own husbands, as unto the Lord. The husband should be next in line after you speak to God every morning. Consult God please! Don't leave the husband hanging by any means. God is the head of man and man is the head of woman. You gave up your own mind when you married and everything must go through your other head…the man. The two of you should operate on one accord. Pray that God will give you the peace of knowing that your husband will ask God for wisdom to lead his family to him, so that you can follow your husband without restraint. When God grants you his peace, you will be free in your spirit and mind to do God's will and submit yourself to your own husband. If you intend to do it God's way, you must submit to your own husband, not the preacher, the boss or friend. The husband is next in your line of authority after God. And I can tell you right now, if you will not let God humble you and prepare your heart, you will never surrender to anyone. You will soon find yourself fighting against God himself. Go figure the spirit behind why you don't want to submit to your husband is that you will not submit to God or anyone else. It is possible to believe that you may be a rebel and may need to ask God to make you over again.

This scripture (verse 22) is touchy to me because, I come from a line of women who did not submit to anyone. Not God, the police, the preacher, the husband, the boss, not anybody. I learned how to be a rebel without a cause early. My grandmother was a firecracker and didn't take orders from anybody. Anyone that tried to defy my grandmother would either get the knife or the piece of steel. My mother was the same way when I was growing up. She would fight at the drop of a hat, and would often drop the hat just to fight. (Quote from Bishop C. Jones) My mother would fight big, small, man or woman. She might not win, but it was a fight. Thank God my mom is in a good marriage now. Thank you Jesus for the grace of God that spared her, saved her and changed her heart. The husband she has now is a God fearing man, patient and kind. He still catches the blunt of some of what she endured in previous relationships, but with a stern talking to, I can encourage her to straighten up. She often says that she learned a lot from me about being a submissive wife. I promise you, nothing that has happened in my life, happened without God's divine intervention. My situation was a unique one, I met William the summer I turned 15. We became friends and he was the perfect gentleman. I never would have thought in a million years that he would have been my husband. I was too young to be interested in boys, let alone a husband.

William often says that the first time he saw me, he told his friends, "That's going to be my wife." That lets you know that men have motives for you the minute they see you. I did like him a lot as a friend, but I was interested in someone else at the time. Little did I know that someone else was also interested in someone else and it was not me. I had no guidance or direction for a boyfriend, much less a husband. But God, through his infinite wisdom, saved me from a world of lust and whoredom and brought me a husband. He has worked to make me happy every day we have been together. I always knew that I was going to be a good wife and mother; I had prayed and asked God to allow me to settle down and be a good wife and mother. I had seen too much with these precious eyes not to be affected in a negative way and live to tell about it. The world had a lot to offer the young girls I grew up with. Many turned to drugs, older men, married men and partying. But it was God! Who is rich in mercy and grace that set me aside for

William. We have had our trials and tribulations, but I am proud to call him my husband. He was a good catcher and he is still seeking God for his wife and family after 24 years of marriage. All I can say is Glory to God in the highest and Hallelujah to his name!

23-For the husband is the head of the wife, even as Christ is the head of the church: and is the savior of the body. 24- Therefore as the church is subject unto Christ, so let the wives be to their own husbands in everything. Just as the church is subject unto the rules and commandments of Christ, the wife must be willing to follow the Godly ways that a man will set up his home. A man will have a way he wants his home scene set up and his children raised. A wife will have to comply or be out of the will of God. But remember, he is following God and surly will not do anything to hurt you or your family. The man still has to be directly accountable to God. So, follow a man who is following God with a submissive woman at his side, and I will show you one successful marriage.

William says that the only man a woman really respects is Jesus because they fear his wrath." Wives be subject to your husbands in everything." I didn't make that one up, it's in the word. You will just have to consult God on that one and I don't think he's changing his mind about it.

25-Husbands, love your wives, even as Christ also loved the church, and gave himself for it: 26-That he might sanctify and cleanse it with the washing of the water by the word.

27- That he might present it to himself a glorious church, not having spot, or wrinkle, or any such thing; but that it should be holy and without blemish. 28- So ought men to love their wives as their own bodies. He that loveth his wife loveth himself. 29- For no man ever yet hated his own flesh; but nourisheth and cherisheth it even as the Lord the church: 30- For we are members of his body, of his flesh, and of his bones.

31-For this cause shall a man leave his father and mother, and shall be joined unto his wife, and they two shall be one flesh. 32-This is a great mystery but I speak concerning Christ and the Church. 33-Nevertheless, let every one of you in particular so love his wife as himself; and the wife see that she reverence her husband.

Presentation

My first thought is how the bride (church) will be presented back to Christ. First, the church has to give up something to follow Christ. Likewise, the wife must also give up something to follow her husband. She must give up her name. No church ever commits to Christ and keeps the world's standards. The wife must give up her self just as the church has to take on the name of Jesus. Genesis 3:16(KJV) Unto the woman he said, I will greatly multiply thy sorrow and thy conception; in sorrow thou shall bring forth children; and thy desire (wants, wishes, requests) shall be to thy husband and he shall rule over thee."

Back in olden days, homes were structured by the Christian example. There was no question that the man was the head of the house. If a man resided in the house and he was the husband and father, he was the head of that house. Modern day Christians have changed the truth of God into a lie. Roles have been reversed and new ideals have invaded the Christian homes of today. Sadly enough, Christians were not notified that God has not changed his mind about the structure of the Christian home. The Church is built on

Christian principles and so should every marriage be built on those same principles.

When I began to assess how God wanted a man to love his wife, I turned to my husband and this conversation continued for two weeks. It is his belief that God intended for a man to protect her, lead her in prayer, seeking God for his family's health, wealth and wisdom. God expects every man to provide for his wife and be a Godly example for his children. Jesus paid the ultimate price for his church and a man should never put a price tag on what his wife is worth. She should be a held close to him, as his prized possession. She should be held in his arms and placed on the top shelf as his trophy. On that note, "No man wants to walk on eggshells with cotton in his shoes."(Mr. Burnside) A woman should make her home conducive for his love. She must be available and free in her spirit and mind to love her man.

2nd Corinthians 3:17 (KJV) "Now the Lord is that Spirit: and where the spirit of the Lord is, there is Liberty." A man should feel free in his own home and not have to walk on eggshells for his wife or children. If a Christian woman does not line up with the word of God for her marriage, she is out of line with God and disobedient to his word. 1st Samuel 15:23 (KJV) " For rebellion is as the sin of witchcraft, and stubbornness is as iniquity and idolatry." Witchcraft is a controlling spirit and has no place in a Christian marriage. Mr. Burnside assessed the opinion of 10 men who agree that women as a whole are not obedient to the word of God when it relates to marriage.

When this witchcraft spirit comes into a marriage, it has the potential to reduce a man's self worth and self esteem. I would like to believe that it is every man's desire to please his wife. However, a man must be built up in his home if he is to survive out in the treacherous world where he is under subjection to so many other forces of authority that govern what he can and cannot accomplish in his life and for his family.

A husband is given a great responsibility over his wife and children. He should make every possible provision for them. They should not be overtaken by the things that others possess by desiring the possessions of his neighbor. This begins by having a budget and not living above the means of your own household. God requires a standard for finances also. This is not a chapter on finances, but most men believe that making a woman happy starts in the wallet. Most women, even if they grew up dirt poor are looking for a man who can given them diamonds and pearls. The breakdown begins when the wife eyes the prizes her neighbor has and pressures the husband. The children also begin to pressure the mother for things of the world that they desire and the mother with her emotional heart for her children begins to spill this cup in the husbands' lap. The husband begins to feel guilty for not being able to provide for his family like old Joe Blow next door and petitions God to move him from a job he loves, a home he built and a community that he gives back to. Before you know it, the husband and wife are working overtime to pay for things they don't have time to enjoy, kids they never see, neighbors that are not impressed and the marriage goes downhill.

This example is precisely why a man should follow God so closely that the Holy Ghost will reveal those things he has in store for him and his family. Jeremiah 29:11(KJV) "I know the thoughts I think toward you, saith the Lord, thoughts of peace, and not evil, to give you an expected end." Above all else, God is concerned with our attitude. The abundance or the lack of money does not affect our relationship with Him, only our attitude does. The Christian must be able to trust God in every circumstance, believing that He loves us and gives us only the stewardship we can handle without being tempted beyond that which we can withstand." (Burkett,L. 1975).

Marriage

M- Master. Trust Him; he has a plan for your marriage.

A- Alpha and Omega. Put him first and last in your marriage and everything in between will work together for your good.

R- Redeemer. He brings life to your marriage.

R- Restorer. He puts everything in its proper place.

I- Immanuel. God is with us in our marriage.

A- Anchor. When we are in trouble, we can hold on to the solid rock.

G- Good Shepherd. He will lead you in your marriage.

E- Everlasting Father. Till death us do part.

(From my friend, Ava Stringfellow)

Pray to God about your marriage every day, trust Him to guide you through your decisions, wait patiently on God to answer your prayer. Respect each other in everything. Love each other unconditionally. Ephesians 3:20 (KJV) "Now unto him that is able to do exceeding; abundantly above all that we ask or think, according to the power that worketh in us" for your marriage also.

It is so amazing to see how much planning goes into selecting wedding rings, picking out the wedding gown and colors and planning a formal reception. However, very little planning goes into planning past the consummating of the marriage bed. I often wonder if the guest would get all dressed up and spend money on a gift if they knew you were not going to stay married past a year or two? Most people take more time planning the actual wedding ceremony than they do getting to know the person they vowed to spend the rest of their life with. I do not think that Christians need to spend years in engagement due to the fact that temptation will definitely arise. However, I do believe that a sufficient amount of time should be allowed to get to know each other and how you each interact in the presence of immediate family members. Seeing a potential partner interact with their family can bring a lot of skeletons out of the closet. If they just happen to be hiding anything, it is sure to surface at some time or another through a family member who feels that it is their business to help you out.

The lust of the flesh and pride of life has trapped many people into saying things at the altar they never intended to fulfill. A person with no character will not be able to keep promises to you or anyone else. With this being said, by all means please seek Godly counsel before entering into the Holy Covenant called Marriage.

Unity

Whoever said, "marriage is a two way street", obviously did not realize that they would have to walk together. Amos 3:3 (KJV) "how can two walk together except they be agreed." On a two way street, traffic is going in opposite directions. That has absolutely no place in a successful marriage. The devil is out to do everything he can to make sure you are always in disagreement with your mate. He pulls out every obstacle imaginable to trip you up. His magnifying glass is so big; he makes even the smallest issues gigantic. Ephesians 4:2&3 (KJV) "With all lowliness and meekness, with long suffering, forbearing one another in love; Endeavoring to keep the unity of the spirit in the bond of peace." He is talking about us, the Christians that are called to keep the peace, even in marriage.

Psalms 34:13 & 14 (KJV) "Keep thy tongue from evil and thy lips from speaking guile. Depart from evil, seek peace, and pursue it.

Psalms 19:14 (KJV) "Let the words of my mouth and the meditations of my heart be acceptable in thy sight, O lord, my strength, and my redeemer."

It is alright if we have an opinion and agree to disagree. But while we must bring the real issues into perspective, the word says in Ephesians 4:26&27 (KJV) "Be ye angry, and sin not; let not the sun go down upon your wrath: Neither give place to the devil." When we have a disagreement and cannot come to an agreement on the matter, we allow sin to creep in and the devil gets a say in how we treat each other. We invite in the demon of stubbornness. We then play the game of "whoever gives in first loses". But the truth of the matter is, whoever gives in first is the wiser person. Never allow the enemy to take a matter to the extreme. Proverbs 10:12 says," hatred stirreth up strife: but love covereth all sins." There is nothing that God and his infinite love for us cannot fix. God is love and you cannot love God and yet not handle a matter with love and understanding.

There will be times when you will not always agree. This only means that you have your own brain and it is working. It also means that you have a will and that will is influenced by your emotions, thoughts and beliefs. No one has to always be right. But we must agree that we will disagree at times but must get it right in order to be in a right standing with God. Some couples want to settle everything in front of the preacher. Let the man of God get some rest and for God's sake grow up and stop whining because you don't get your way. If you go back to the word, "submitting yourselves to each other in the fear of God", we both agree to win this fight together on our knees. We put the devil to an open shame when we agree to let go of the small stuff. God is pleased when we handle a matter decently and orderly. Christians do not allow disagreements to become grudges, but disagreements in the Christian marriage should become discussions. Settle matters quickly and stay in good standing with God.

Worship should be at the forefront of unifying a marriage and home. Worship should be done together. There is no "my church, your church". God said in his word, Ephesians 4:5(KJV) "One Lord, one faith and one baptism." Therefore, a home should have one place of worship. There is no reason that couples with two different faiths or religions should believe that their union will survive. 2nd Corinthians 6:14 (KJV) "Be ye not unequally yoked together with unbelievers: for what fellowship hath righteousness with unrighteousness? And what communion hath light with darkness." All I am saying is that there will always be conflict where spiritual things do not line up. It is a known fact that Baptist and Pentecostals do not share the same denominational views, neither Catholic nor Methodists.

I am not saying that you do not believe in God. I am saying that the method in which you believe will not be equal. While one believes it does not take much effort to serve God, the other may believe in an all out worship and praise celebration. It can become offensive to a person for his or her God not to be honored in the fashion in which they deem appropriate. I would not advise you to try it knowing what the word of God says about it. If you do, just know up front that the devil will unleash an all out war against religion and God and you both may decide to ride worship out at the house. This is equally wrong, because Hebrews 10:25 (KJV) "Not forsaking the assembling of ourselves together, as the manner of some is; but exhorting one another: and so much the more as ye see the day approaching." God is saying that attending the House of Prayer, which is his church, should be done more and more, and even more as Jesus' coming gets closer.

We need to meet on a regular basis with believers of our own faith so that we may be encouraged in the faith. Tradition will kill a marriage. No more doing things my own way. We have become "One twain flesh". St. Mark 3:25 (KJV) "And if a house be divided against itself, that house cannot stand. I would like to borrow a phrase from my dear husband, "one thing for certain and two things for sure, 1. God's word is true. 2. It works for every situation. Believe this, God has every base covered. Man makes many loop holes through his word to fit his own selfish desires. But God's word will never change.

My Best Friend

It is a good thing to actually like the person you are married to. I have heard people say, "I love you, but I don't like you all the time." Why should this statement be an issue in a marriage? You work eight to twelve hours a day on a job and tolerate your co-workers, but when you come home you have nothing to talk about. This is a very puzzling thing to me. Why would you choose a mate to spend your life with, share your love, joys, failures and victories, and not attempt to build a happy home with them?

Amos 3:3(KJV) "Can two walk together, except they be agreed?" This scripture is usually used in unison with the old adage, "birds of a feather flock together." It obvious that you had something in common at one time with the one you married. You will just have to build on the particular thing that brought you together. Far too many times, our flesh has dictated our destiny and we end up in a world of trouble and then try to justify our getting out. Just recognize that God will not take it lightly that you entered into his covenant blinded by your flesh. This is why sexual purity and moral ethics are a big part of how God structured his church. He knew that we would be drawn away by our fleshly desires. God said in 1ˢᵗ Corinthians 6:18 (KJV) "Flee fornication, every sin that a man does is without the body; but he that committeth fornication sinneth against his own body. 19- What? Know ye not that your body is the temple of the Holy Ghost which is in you, which ye have of God, and you are not your own? 20- For you are bought with a price: therefore glorify God in your body, and in your spirit, which are God's."

When God spoke on celibacy and marriage, he said in Amos 7:1-9.(KJV) 1-Now concerning the things, whereof ye wrote unto me: It is good for a man not to touch a woman. 2-Nevertheless, to avoid fornication, let every man have his own wife, and let every woman have her own husband. 3-Let the husbands render unto his wife due benevolence: and likewise also the wife unto the husband. 4-The wife hath not power of her own body, but the husband and likewise also the husband hath not power of his own body, but the wife. 5-Defraud ye not one the other, except it be with consent for a time, that ye may give yourself to fasting and prayer; and come together again, that Satan tempt you not for your continency. 6-But I speak this by permission, and not of commandment. 7-For I would that all men were even as I myself. But every man hath his proper gift of God, one after this manner, and another after that. 8-I say therefore to the unmarried and widows, it is good for them to abide even as I. 9-But if they cannot contain, let them marry: for it is better to marry than to burn. God is all for marriage between a man and a woman. Marriage should not be entered into half heartedly. Marriage may take a lifetime to master, but entering in should take careful consideration and prayer.

Hebrew 13:14 "Marriage is honorable in all, and the bed undefiled: but whoremongers and adulterers God will judge." We should not allow our sex organs to decide who we marry.

You should never allow the desires of your flesh to dictate the destiny of your soul. You will be held accountable as to how you treated your husband or wife. You do not need to worry about how they treat you. That part is for God to handle and believe me, he will. The only part of the marriage that you can control is how you behave in it. Romans 14:12 (KJV) So then every one of us shall give an account of himself to God." While we are choosing a mate, let's allow God to be in control and not our flesh. I said all of that, just to say this. Marriage will Always represent Christ and his church. This is why it is so important to treat your marriage according to the word of God. Christians must make a conscience effort to rise up above situations that sinner's just breeze through. God knows that we will encounter difficulty on this journey with him. Here is a reminder, if you are walking with God, you cannot go wrong. Bishop Jones use to teach us that there are some things we think we cannot go through at times, but some sinners are going to stand up in judgment against us. Christians are so thin-skinned, sensitive and just outright wimps when it comes to upholding the word of God. It is time for the true Christians to come up. I am not saying that you should allow anything to transpire in your marriage and you take it. I am simply saying if the word of God is not fitting for your problem, maybe you should not be married. However, I have not found any issue too big for God. Jeremiah 32:37 (KJV) "Behold, I am the Lord, the God of all flesh: is there anything too hard for me? Jeremiah 32:17 (KJV) "Ah Lord God! Behold thou hast made the heaven and the earth by thy great power and stretched out arm, and there is nothing too hard for thee:"

Most people rely on how they feel about things that happen in their marriage to dictate their love for their mate. Marriage is spiritual before it is emotional. Although all aspects of a marriage are of great importance, how you feel on a certain day has nothing to do with how you should treat your mate or value the covenant of marriage.

Sometimes we can't see the forest for the trees. We tend to think someone else has it better than we do. I am privileged to say that I believe I have one of the best husbands God ever created. I can say this because my husband recognizes that he was created in the likeness of God. He acknowledges Jesus as his personal savior and seeks everyday to be more like him. I can live a long time on that. It is my belief that a man that will not seek the Lord, will chase after anything. As a wife, I must understand that I will never be able to compete with a man. Any woman that thinks she can compete with a man is in for a rude awakening.

I heard Dr. James Dobson say, "Anything with no head is dead and anything with two heads is a freak." A woman can never lead herself to believe that she is the man and the woman of the house. If the husband is not doing his part to lead the wife and family to Christ, he is out of line with God. 1st Corinthians 11:3 (KJV) "But I would have you know, that the head of every man is Christ: and the head of the woman is the man: and the head of Christ is God." His word is true and every home should be governed accordingly. Remember that God commanded that man should love his wife as Christ loved the Church and this is some awesome love. Thank God for his example of agape love. Unconditional, fulfilled and selfless love has no boundaries. Think about not catering to yourself, but to each other. No one goes lacking following this method of love.

The Roller Coaster Of Love

Remember when you were a child and you got to go to the county fair or some fancy theme park? When your parents told you that they were taking you, you were so excited. You could hardly contain yourself. You were up all night before in anticipation of the fun you would have. When your parents told you that you could invite a friend you really got excited. You were going on an exciting trip and got to bring a friend. Wow, what a time we will have. You already knew you would have so much fun. The next day, you arrive at the park with your family and friend. You are exited, anxious and happy to be there. You pull your friend from one ride to the next, filling up on cotton candy and candied apples. Your parents take lots of pictures, you make great memories. As the day draws to a close, you are sad, but thrilled at the time you had.

It seems that you and your friend had a great time at the park. The only regret you have is that you were not allowed to stay longer. You wished you had one more ride, just one more snack. There was not enough time in one day to do all you intended to do with your friend. But you will have a great story to tell, some souvenirs and great memories.

Consider this situation that relates to God and marriage. How do you think God would feel when we arrive at the roller coaster of life and marriage? We arrive hand in hand with our friend, the absolute love of our life. If someone would tell us that this relationship is not real, we would not listen. We have already made up our own mind. We did not ask permission to take this ride, we arrived alone and we are on the ride of a lifetime.

We arrive at the amusement park called life. We stand in a long line called commitment, purchase a ticket at the altar of love and commit to going on a long ride called marriage with our friend. We recognize that once we get on the roller coaster, we are locked end for the duration. There is no getting off until the controller (God) says so. The roller coaster called marriage takes you on a high like no other. All eyes are on you and your friend. Spectators on the ground are standing by with the expectation that you will indeed finish the race. The spectators are expecting the same thrill they think you are having when they get on.

The roller coaster eases off its starting mark and around a slow curve. By the time you get a real grip on the ride, the butterflies turn into an ill feeling. You know what's coming next. The deep dips of finances take a seat, front row and center. Next, the side sharp curve of raising kids, and the steep hill of your careers, family and friends. Lastly, we find ourselves at the pinnacle of our marriage. We are up so high that our view is cloudy. Stop, for one moment. You have reached the top, hands in the air—wheeee! You feel like you are on top of the world. You may even have a snapshot taken at the top. Of course, you want to remember this very moment. You can look back and see how far you have come. But, turn around; you still have so much farther to go. Wow! Part two is about to begin. Talk about jitters, you can't get off.

At this point in the ride, all you can think about is the story you will have to tell. The only way you can tell others how much fun you've had is if you get to the end. Remember the people you left on the ground? They are still waiting and watching to see if you will make off intact. Look out now, what in the world is really going on? Somebody wants off at a pivotal point of the ride. Buddy, you can't get off mid air. That wasn't in the plan. OK, go ahead, get off and you're headed for disaster city. As scared, anxious and uncertain as it may seem, you will have to finish this course. Do you remember you purchased a ticket and committed to take a ride? You chose to get on and be locked in. You had every opportunity to change your mind while you were waiting in line. But, you stood there at the altar and allowed the vows to go forth. Hand in hand you agreed, until death do we part. The only way you can get off the roller coaster now is jump off. God said death will release you. Sadly, you will never be able to tell your story. There is no victory in quitting. You were just a taker, not an endurer. You really only wanted the quick thrill. Chances are you were already thinking about the next ride while trying to get off of the rollercoaster. Remember, the ride is only successful if you endure until the end. Until death do we part?

I remember in 2007 we took our children to Disney World for my daughter's high school graduation. Our first stop was Universal Studios. We got there early. We didn't have to stand in any long line yet. My husband, daughter and I took a mad dash for the roller coaster. It was called the "The Incredible Hulk". My son decided early on that he was not going. We finally got on the ride, we strapped in. My husband and daughter got in front and I occupied in the back seat. The ride started off wild and crazy. They took it high, they took it low. We flipped upside down, over the top and round again. Then, midway, I heard my daughter scream,

"There's the camera, look! I did not remember looking up at this point in the ride. But pictures do not lie.

We made it off of the roller coaster, thank God. We stood in line to see our picture. I was really surprised to see that at the moment my daughter said "look, there's the camera"; I had only raised my head slightly and opened one eye.

I obviously missed the thrill and rode with my eyes shut. God is taking snap shots of our lives and evaluating how we treat his covenant. You cannot go through a marriage with "one eye open like you're winking" (Will B.) Again, this covenant should not be entered into lightly. Open your eyes honey. Know what is going on, participate, converse, relate and don't hesitate to be present every day. God is looking and he is anxiously waiting for the report of a good Christian marriage.

Divorce

This is a subject that I have not experienced personally. What I say here is divinely given through prayer and seeking God for wisdom. Divorce is not an option for the Christian marriage. It is a circumstantial choice. God never intended for divorce to be an issue in marriage. The divine ideal for marriage is clearly a life-long bond that unites husband and wife in a "one flesh" relationship. Genesis 2:24 (KJV) In the book of St Matthew when the Pharisees came unto Jesus to question him about "putting away one's wife", V-4-9 says Jesus answered and said unto them, "Have you not read, that he which made them at the beginning made them male and female, And said, for this cause shall a man leave father and mother, and shall cleave to his wife: and they twain shall be one flesh? Wherefore, they are no more twain, but one flesh. What therefore God has joined together, let no man put asunder."

The Pharisees continued to press Jesus, "Why did Moses then command to give a writing of divorcement, and to put her away? Jesus then said unto them," Moses because of the hardness of your hearts suffered you to put away your wives: but from the beginning it was not so. And I (Jesus) say unto you, except it be for fornication, and shall marry another, committeth adultery: and whoso marrieth her which is put away doth commit adultery."

I have heard people say, "God did not put us together". Maybe God did not put you together, but since you are already joined, I assure you that God can keep you together. When we are married, we need to consider that spiritual warfare is a real thing. When you start warring against each other, the devil takes a front row seat. He is enjoying the shows we put on for him and his demons. The devil then commits a bold act, pointing his finger in the face of God and laughing saying, "look at them". "They are killing each other, stealing their family's legacy and ultimately destroying their families." I believe when it is all over, and the divorce papers are signed, the devil stamps his seal of approval on it. "MISSION ACCOMPLISHED!"

Hebrews 13:4 (KJV) "Marriage is honorable in all, and the bed undefiled: but whoremongers and adulterers God will judge." Marriage vows are sacred when spoken in the sight of God and witnesses. It is a promise or oath, a binding promise, one by which a person is bound. God requires vows of marriage to be upheld until death unless you choose the circumstantial option. I don't doubt there are many reasons not to stay in a marriage. I just hope the one that wants out stays in the will of the Lord while they are on their way out. Tyler Perry had a good point when he wrote "Why did I get married?" This is not exactly a good question to be asking when you get in it. Everyone is not meant for marriage, some are called to be in the singles ministry and continue in the work of God until he comes. However, many do not seek him long enough to know whether marriage is for them or not. This race is not for the faint hearted.

The church has a different responsibility in marriage than the world. The example of marriage was established in the beginning. The maturity and responsibility of creating a successful marriage is in the hands of the Christian. Sound character and integrity of marriage should be an example of a Christian marriage.

Hebrews 13:4 (New Living Translation) "Give honor to marriage and remain faithful to one another in marriage. God will surely judge people who are immoral and those who commit adultery."

Hebrews 13:4 (Amplified Bible) "Let marriage be held in honor (esteemed, worthy, precious, of great price, and especially dear) in all things. And thus let the marriage bed be undefiled (kept undishonored); for God will judge and punish the unchaste (all guilty of sexual vice) and adulterers."

Some of our most prominent televangelists are listed among those who have chosen divorce as an option out of marriage. I will not be the first to judge why the decision came about. God only approved one exception, but men have made many exceptions to the rule and are preaching a word that will not stand up in heaven. Saints do not have irreconcilable differences. Saints do not have blowouts. There are slow leaks along the way that were not fixed in time. It is only obvious that someone stepped outside the gate to take a look and stayed to long. Someone stepped outside of the will of God. You say you made a blunder, but that is what repentance is for. Repent, not Repeat. Some say we should allow Pastors and ministers to be human. There is absolutely no way that you or I can make them immortal or untouchable, but they must be held to a higher calling in Christ Jesus or else they make a mockery or monkey out of the Gospel of truth.

The fact of the matter is that there are just some places you will not be able to go. There will be some people you will not be able to entertain and some things you will not be able to do. For the sake of the Gospel, you must keep your record clean. Romans 14: 16 (KJV) "Let not then your good be evil spoken of:" If it is offensive to the body of Christ, don't do it. Sure, you are in charge; you are the one who has the rule over them. But you are subject to rebel and step out of line at any time. Then after it's all said and done and you have to be rebuked by your peers, dragged back into the gate, you're mad. It's better to be mad than embarrassed by the devil.

The world can make divorce look so appealing. It becomes contagious to the onlookers. Misery really does love company. The influence that celebrities and the world have on the church is overwhelming. The church is quick to pick up this copycat spirit and adopt the standards of the world. The church needs to get a grip, deal with the issues in their home. Divorce is spreading like a wildfire in the church. I continue to say that sometimes there is nothing that you can do to stop it. If a person wants to walk away, you have to let it be. But by all means God is able to keep you if you desire keeping. Jude 24 (KJV) "Now unto him that is able to keep you from falling, and to present you faultless before the presence of his glory with exceeding joy. "

Alternative Life Styles

In the beginning, God created them male and female. Genesis 1:27-28. (KJV) "So God created man in his own image, in the image of God created he him; male and female created he them. And God said unto them, be fruitful and multiply, and replenish the earth, and subdue it:" This command alone tells us that marriage is and always will be between a man and a woman. There is no judge, jury or senate living that has the boldness to look God in the eye and tell him he did not mean what he said. There will never ever be a law written that will change the truth of God into a lie. Leviticus 20:13 (KJV) "If a man also lies with mankind, as he lieth with a woman, both of them have committed an abomination: they shall surely be put to death: their blood shall be upon them." There are many sexual encounters that Leviticus lists that are wrong, but I am addressing homosexuality at this time.

I am trying to make it plain. I don't want anyone reading this book to get it twisted. What I am saying is there will never be a legal, moral, ethical or same sex marriage between two individuals of the same sex that will stand up in heaven. Homosexuality is a spirit that must be dealt with just like any other demonic perpetrator. Homosexuality is an unruly evil that has crept up in the minds of men and women and deceived them into believing that it is alright to practice acting out the role of something that your imagination dreamed up. Homosexuality exalts itself against the knowledge of God. Some would rather remain ignorant than to the fact that a square peg just will not fit into a round circle hole. My Bishop use to say, "If you are confused about your gender, or if you are a man or woman, look down there and see what tools you were given and you have your answer." Certain tools accomplish certain jobs. Hammers don't drill holes and skil saws do not hammer nails. What are you working with?

Genesis 13:13 (KJV) "But the men of Sodom, (hence the term sodomy) were wicked and sinners before the Lord exceedingly.

Genesis 19:4 (New Living Translation) "Before the night was over, all the men of Sodom, young and old came to Lot's house and asked him, "where are the men who came to spend the night? Bring them out to us so that we may have sex with them." The men of Sodom were seeking the angels that came to deliver a message to Lot.

Genesis 19:6 (NLT) Lot begged them to leave and offered his daughters to them to have as they pleased. He told the homosexual men "the men in his house were his guest and were under his protection."

Genesis 19:9 (NLT) the men shouted "Stand Back, you came here as an outsider and now you're trying to judge us." The men lunged at Lot and the angels pulled Lot back into the house.

Genesis 19:12 (NLT) finally the angels told Lot God's plan to destroy the city of Sodom and Gomorrah. The angels ask, "Do you have any relatives here? Get everybody out, you and your family. The cry against this place is so great it has reached the Lord and sent us to destroy it."

Lot procrastinated about leaving Sodom. The angels practically had to throw him out. What was it about Sodom that Lot loved so much? Perhaps a little bit of sodomy in his spirit? After Lot finally got out of the city, the Lord rained down fire and burning sulfur. Likewise, God will ultimately replay this same scenario in our society very soon. God promised Noah that the rainbow in the clouds was his sign that he would never again cover the earth with water. So with that said, it won't be water but fire next time. Singing, "it's gonna rain, it's gonna rain. God showed Noah, the rainbow sign; he said it won't be water, but fire next time." We were singing that one in the children's choir when I was 10 years old. We can keep singing because it won't change.

The devil would have God's people to see images of homosexual couples on TV and the internet carrying on as if they were married. Some Homosexual couples even have the audacity to adopt children. This still does not make them mother or father to them. But the suggestion is to implant the seed in the mind of our children to make them think it is ok to have two moms or two dads. The homosexual couples train their kids to tell others when questioned that the reason they have two dads is that they are special. Well that is true, a special case for the Lord to rain fire from heaven on. The enemy would like to have marriage between a man and a woman annulled in the sight of God, by trying to prove that homosexuals deserve the same rights in marriage as God gave to Adam and Eve. Those men and women in authority in the White House, Congress and the local court houses who agree with the devil and marry two of the same sex will have to give an account to a just God. And that will be a day of reckoning. God is not going to apologize to Sodom and Gomorrah for allowing America to walk away free. It just will not happen. These examples were left on record for us as an inspiration to walk in truth. Every man and woman will have to give an account for every deed done in their body. "We must get it right or get left." (She'Keena A. Burnside's quote)

Five Risky Marriage Types

1. Selfish people- display a very uncaring attitude and a strong "me first" characteristic. They put themselves first and their needs only. They only give attention to their priorities, their goals and in the process do not even realize that other people are really being affected. A selfish person would consider others only as a means to get what benefits them. They have a tunnel vision which starts from and leads to themselves and their personal needs. Selfish people do not share or care for others needs. It is always a conflict to see another's ideas as a real issue. Selfish people may be corporate entertainers and only care for those who have the power to fulfill their personal desires and elevate them in terms of material, financial and spiritual realms. Selfish people are insecure and are not team players. They are highly self-centered and self obsessed.

Oscar Wilde, the Irish poet states (Selfish people)
"There are many things that we would throw away if we were not afraid that others might pick them up"

2. Manipulative people- These types of people are your schemers and plotters. This characteristic arises from the fact that they are driven by the loss of control. They want to control everything by maligning someone's reputation or by misrepresenting things. Manipulative people tend to influence others skillfully in an unfair manner. They butter you up, make you feel guilty about not giving in to their needs. These people usually sound like a broken record, speaking in a convincing, coercing tone. Bullying is often a tactic and they only have selective memory. They always remember what they sacrifice for you, but never admit to the tyranny they put you through to get what they want. This witchcraft spirit would control the very elect if at all possible. Their suggestions are controlling and often change your plans so subtly; you don't even notice that you are off of your course and following them.

3. Mean Spirited- This type of person is usually the one who has been abused or bullied in some form or fashion. They have a malicious, petty spirit. They usually bully others psychologically and physically. They are aggressive, angry and mean. They are the "chickens on the yard that see blood and get to pecking at the injured chicken" they show "no mercy". Mean-Spirited people tend to be afraid and use their bullying to control others. They are almost always bluffing their prey into believing they are tough and could care less how they feel. But the true essence of their character is hidden in some

type of hurt or disappointment. Mean-Spirited people need help that they are too proud to seek. In this case, pray for the spirit and heart of this person to be changed and the inner man will ultimately give in.

4. Sensitive- This type of person may process sensory data much more deeply and thoroughly due to a biological difference in their nervous system. This type is often confused, shy and has social anxiety. Sensitive people's feelings are very fragile. They are the easiest to become offended. They over analyze every situation and build big mountains out of mole hills. Sensitive people hold grudges for long periods of time. They do not build relationships quickly and tend to shy away from social gatherings. Sensitive people tend to be very insecure. Sensitive people would rather be alone and not have to deal with others opinions or suggestions of others. They do not work well in group settings. They require much encouragement to make it through what may seem like an average day to others. They do not make their needs known. They assume everyone knows their needs and they are just being overlooked. They may need you to hold their hand on a regular basis and surly will need tender loving care often. Sensitive people may be tearful often and may end up in depression. A Close watch is advised.

5. Jealous- Jealousy is an emotion that typically refers to the negative thoughts and feelings of insecurity, fear and anxiety over an anticipated

loss of something the person values. Such as relationships, friendships or loves. Jealousy often consists of a combination of emotions such as anger, sadness and disgust. It is not to be confused with Envy. Envy (invidiousness) is an emotion that often occurs when a person does not possess another person's superior quality, achievement or material possession and desires it or wishes that the other person did not have it. Envy is the same as Covetousness. Remember, "thou shall not covet". It is a distorted negative perception. Envy and Jealousy are often interchangeable, but stand for two different distinct emotions. Jealous people can be "accusers of the brethren". Jealousy wastes time and energy. If we trust in the Lord and not to man, we have no room for insecurities.

All five of these negative traits are those that the Lord says are highly ineffective in marriages. They spin the wheels of productivity out of motion. They go against the grain. They push against the will of God in every aspect. Many times in marriage, we are not fighting against the person we are married to but against spirits that wage war against the flesh. These negative traits are born of the flesh, devil and the world. They are the fruits of the enemy. "The fruit of God's Spirit is love, joy, peace, longsuffering, gentleness, goodness, faith, meekness, temperance." Galatians 5:22-23. (KJV)

The Only "I" Allowed In Marriage

1. Invest means to devote morally or psychologically, for a purpose; to commit to. This definition fits marriage perfectly. Investing in a marriage takes effort. You will not reap where you have not sown. It kind of reminds me of people who try to beat checks to the bank. You know you have not put any money in the bank, and still write checks for things you cannot pay for. It is not a good thing to leave the bank of marriage empty. If someone else comes along and makes an investment, it is possible that they will reap of the emotional love and time that you are legally entitled to. Sometimes, not investing in our mate can leave the door open for temptation. Fulfillment in marriage comes from investing quality time, intellectual conversation and sensual affection. Love is actually spelled T-I-M-E. I hear what you're saying, I see what you're buying, but I need you to invest some time with me. There is a great return on the investment in marriage. One hundred fold is

waiting from the investment you place in your marriage. Calls and text messages throughout the day to say "I love you" are a great way to set the mood. Remember sex does not start in the bedroom. For women, the mood for sex cannot start in the bedroom. It must start emotionally for a woman and must end physically with the man. When the day ends, it is over. Plan some time for intimacy. That is one investment you will not regret.

Galatians 6:9 (KJV) "And let us not be weary in well doing: for in due season we shall reap, if we faint not."

2. Invent- to produce for the first time through the use of the imagination or the ingenious thinking and experiment; devise. Marriage needs refreshing new ideas to remain alive. Invent new ways to spend time together; date night should be a priority. Lunch dates have been added to our marriage. We love our lunch dates, sitting in little corners conversing, laughing and catching up. When our kids were younger, we did picnics with them. Often times, the children may have to come along. But try to make it a priority to schedule time alone. William and I bought the video game "Deal or No Deal" and that's what we play in our spare time. We love it. Incorporate activities you enjoy, visit a museum or go to a concert. You need that special time together. Be open, have fun. Enjoy.

Psalms 18: - "let thy fountain be blessed: and rejoice with the wife of thy youth."

3. Invite means to urge politely, to offer an incentive or inducement to: Entice. Let your mate know that you are available to them. Invite them to the dinner table. Family meals are awesome in our house. Even though are children are grown and in college. If they are home, they live for meal time; it's like an open forum or round table discussion. Invite your mate to bed, just give a stated time. "We're going to bed after we finish watching this show," or "it is our goal to be in bed at 10 pm." Establish some boundaries to make invitations work. Don't make it a habit of bringing work home. Manage your time so that the urging or enticement can be followed through. Do not make it a habit of missing invitations. It is amazing how many couples are lonely and sleep together every night. Loneliness is not a good thing. Fulfill your mates' invitation by winding down, getting a warm bath or shower and clearing your mind. Bring your whole self in to share with your mate.

Psalms 5:15 "Drink water from your own well, share your love only with your wife."

4. Initiate- to cause or facilitate the beginning of: set going. Innovate. After inviting, you must initiate. There is no excuse for positive things not happening in a marriage. Dates, vacations, family meetings, intimate encounters are needed to make a marriage functional. Do not wait on your mate to initiate all the time. Spontaneity keeps a marriage alive. Keep the wheels turning

in motion. Standstills are ultimately death. I remember when William use to work the graveyard shift; he would go in at six pm and come home at four am. At least once a week, I would go to bed early so I could be rested when he got home in the morning. After he would get his shower, I would have a light breakfast laid out on a blanket in the bedroom. It was almost like a picnic and so much fun. You have to do things that keep the honeymoon alive. After 24 years of marriage, I still love spending time with him and we have so much fun together. We both initiate and we both benefit equally from investing special times in our marriage.

Songs of Solomon 6:2-3 (KJV) "My beloved has gone down to his garden, to the bed of spices, to feed in the gardens and to gather lilies. V-3 "I am my beloved's (garden) and my beloved is mine! He feeds among the lilies (which grow there).

This woman made it plain. The garden is my man and he is initiating a plan to love me.

5. Intensify- to make more intense; to Strengthen. The height and depth of Love in a marriage can be immeasurable. The intensity of the love and affection should be so strong, nothing can get in. Keep the fires burning by investing, inventing, inviting and initiating in your marriage. Preparing to love is greater than the love itself. Foreplay can lead to more than just sex. Foreplay builds trust, intimacy and ultimately a romance that is strengthened by bonds no one can break. Turning up the heat

in every area leaves no room for foolishness. I always say that my husband has set the bar so high; it would be impossible for another man to compete with him. He takes care of business in every aspect. Finances, taking care of our children, keeping me happy are his ultimate goal. He tells our children that no one eats until I get home from work. He said he is cooking for his wife and they just happen to be here to eat. Wow! He got some points for that one. He let it be known that it is all about me.

Songs of Solomon 6:10-12 (KJV) She proudly says, "I am my beloved and his desire is towards me." V-11 She says, "Come, my beloved! Let us go forth into the field, let us lodge in the villages." V-12 "Let us go out early to the vineyards and see whether the vines have budded, whether the grape blossoms have open and whether the pomegranates are in bloom. There I will give you my love." This is one time you may be allowed to think sort of "in the gutter".

Wow! How sensual, I am ready to love you is what she is saying. All signs point to go. You have prepared a place for me, the atmosphere is right; now let's go get our groove on. That is ultimately what she was saying. He initiated and she responded. Well done.

Co-Habitating

The truth of the matter is, I wanted to call this chapter "Shacking". Most of us know exactly what that is. For those of you who don't, it is living with someone you are not married to and acting as if you are married. The origin of Shacking was actually adopted from the slavery days. On February 27, 1966, "an act of the Virginia General legalized common law marriage among free or enslaved Americans of African descent. The Act was rendered necessary to meet abnormal conditions that existed among the colored race in consequence to the abolition of Negro slavery in the South as a result of the Civil War."

Without this enabling act, slave marriages which were largely obtained among that class of the population were invalid. Being a slave meant that they were incapable of entering into any legal contract, including that of marriage. When therefore these former slaves were emancipated and given to rights and privileges of citizenship, the good order of society demanded that these inchoate marriages should be recognized as lawful and any children born to that couple should be legitimate.

The right of children born to slave marriages to inherit property from the father was regarded of sufficient consequence to be expressly secured both by the Constitution of 1869 and of 1902. The act in question (now section 2227 of the code) declares that "where colored persons prior to February 27, 1866 agreed to occupy the relation of husband and wife were cohabitating together at the date, whether rites of marriage had been celebrated between them or not, they shall be deemed husband and wife. They shall be entitled to the rights and privileges and subject to the duties and obligations to that relation in like manner, as if they had lawfully married; and their children shall be deemed legitimate whether born before or after said date. Where the two parties ceased to cohabitate before February 7, 1866, in the consequence of the death of the woman or from any other cause, all the children of the woman recognized by the man to be his shall be deemed legitimate.

Constitution of Virginia, 1869, section 9, Article 1; and section 195, Act XIV of the present Constitution.

Shacking or living in with someone who you are not married to is a generational curse. It is a mental and physical atrocity. It is a sin in the eyes of God and a blow to the temple of the Holy Ghost. The Constitution and racist leaders of this country decided that African Americans in these United States were not worthy to be viewed as human and therefore could not enter into any contracts. Contracts specifically affecting marriage were off limits to African Americans. Therefore, men and women of the African race saw fit to call common-law marriage legal.

The devil is a liar and deceiver. He continues to keep men and women enslaved to the sins of fornication and adultery from generation to generation. These people even think that they can somehow take on the name of the one they are not legally married to. The old saying goes, "why buy the cow when you can get the milk free?" Men have the nerve to date women five and 10 years and have no specific plans for her but to drag her along. And because she feels so special, she allows him to drag her. He is perhaps waiting for that special moment when God is going to make him rich and a house is going to magically appear and then he'll marry her. Women stop being so naïve and get it together. He doesn't have to eat a whole cow to know its beef. (Bishop Clifton Jones) Remember, I am still directing Christians in the word. There are people professing Christianity and in the name of their fleshly lusts and "God knows they have needs," continue to sleep with women with no intention to commit to them or marry them. Woman! He is using you and you need to get a grip. Don't send your soul to hell fooling around with a piece of meat that cannot give you any Godly gain.

1st Corinthians 6:18- 20 (KJV) "Flee fornication. Every sin that a man does is without the body; but he that commits fornication sins against his own body. What? Do you not know that your body is the temple of the Holy Ghost which is in you, which you have of God, and you are not your own. For you are bought with a price: (the blood of Jesus) therefore glorify God in your body and in your spirit which are Gods".

1st Corinthians 7: 1-2 (KJV) "Now concerning the things whereof you wrote unto me: It is good for a man not to touch a woman. Nevertheless, to avoid fornication, let every man have his own wife, and let every man have his own wife, and let every woman have her own husband."

1st Corinthians 6:13(KJV) "Meats for the belly, and the belly for meats: but God shall destroy both it and them.

Now the body is not for fornication but for the Lord; and the Lord for the body."

Let us therefore honor marriage so that the sanctity of marriage can be restored. No longer be drawn away by your fleshly lusts to satisfy the desires of the flesh, placing you in harm's way. The devil would have you to believe that it is ok as long as you intend to get it right. God is merciful and long suffering, but do not think that you can ever pull the wool over the eyes of God. He sees and knows all. He knows the very intent of the heart. Again I say, get it right or get left. Since our ultimate goal as Christians is to be allowed into heaven, let us live like it. You can always tell where a person is going in the hereafter, by what he goes after here. (Bishop Clifton Jones)

Single Ladies

It is my desire that you live modestly and sober until God brings you the desire of your heart. Make your request known to God. Be realistic, not ridiculous. God is able to bring you a Godly man in due season. Accept nothing but God's best. A man that loves your God is able to love you more than enough. God is a God of more than enough. I am merely carrying on a conversation with you because I am sure we have had this type of conversation before.

While you wait, make yourself presentable to God and him. Make sure you are well groomed. You will only attract the attention of what you are prepared for. If you dress worldly, worldly men will come running. If you dress modestly, men will respect you long before they approach you. Seek the heart of God to know who you are in him. Remember no person can make you happy. Happiness is a state of mind, a pure processing of thoughts sifted by God. Keep your heart in Gods' hands and your head in his word. Pray without ceasing, thanking God for all things. Recognize what the will of God is for your life and be richly blessed in benefits God has for you waiting for your husband.

To My Only Son

Man of honor and valor that's what you are. You already possess a heart from God. I know the woman God has prepared for you will love you because you are easy to love. The passion you have for life and love will take you far. Remember I always told you "Don't see that woman that you can live with, seek the one you refuse to live without. Finding her is a good thing and comes with favor from God. You are a blessing and a joy as a son. Put God first in all that you do and he will direct your path and order your steps. The Key to a blessed life is in his word. Seek God for the plans he has for you. This is the legacy I leave for you as you carry on the family name, know and understand that perfect love you first experienced was with me, your mother. When you find your wife, love her completely as God has love you and you will be a blessing to your wife and children. William Malcolm Burnside, you have been charged to be a blessing to "Mrs. B."

For the Single individual this will be no cake walk. The singles ministry will require more and more is expected. Why? If you say you're in the singles ministry, what exactly does that mean? Well from my perspective, feeding the hungry, clothing the orphans and visiting the widows will take up much more time than pleasure. Of course I know this is a ministry for us all, but ministry will require more from the singles. Singles ministry is not a social club, a trip and eating out. Who are you ministering to? I guess you could say each other. So, I ask the question is single your life long goal or do you desire a companion? If you answered yes to the latter, you will need wise counsel and a deeper understanding of what God requires of you. Marriage brings with it the complexities of many needs. Some of which a single person may not easily adapt to. God knows we have desires for friendship and companionship. The issue arises when we cannot rightly distinguish between the two.

Somewhere, a man is seeking a wife and a woman is waiting for her husband. For a woman to say she is looking for a good man would be out of line with the word of God. The scriptures says, "He that finds a wife finds a good thing and have obtained favor of the Lord." Women, ask yourselves, how good am I? Am I submissive to authority now? Do I have a problem respecting and obeying the head of any organization? Would I call myself a rebel for any cause? Am I aggressive and always wanting my way? (Selfish) Is it your way or the highway? If you answered yes to any of these questions, I need to inform you that marriage is a ministry of servitude. I often have women ask me how it is that I serve my husband is. My answer is that my desire is to him and he rules over me according to God's word in Genesis Chapter 3 v16. My husband is not a hard task master because he loves me unconditionally and he also serves me. One of the keys to a good marriage is serving each other constantly. You say you need some me time? It is now our time and you must sometimes ask to use some of it. God has placed man as the head in order to lead the wife and family to him.

One thing a single person seeking a wife or waiting on their husband must do is pray to God for guidance. If you end up with the wrong rib, hell will not be a place so far away from earth for you. Seek God for direction, he has plans for your life; ask him if marriage is in it for you. God said, "It is not good that man should be alone; I will make him a help mate."

Matthew 6:33(KJV) "But seek ye first the kingdom of God, and his righteousness; and all these things shall be added unto you."

Is this an easy task? I should say not. When you desire anything of the Lord and pray about it, the hardest task is waiting for the Lord's answer. Be encouraged, delayed does not mean denied. Be specific in your requests to God, not ridiculous. God already knows what you need, but he still requires you to ask. Women stop saying I'm looking, and start saying I'm waiting. Looking is out of the will of God. To wait means "to stay, remain." I am not trying to be deep or so prolific that you will not be able to grasp just simple concepts to just being who God wants you to be.

Don't accept the first thing running through because of your desperation for a mate. God makes no mistakes and he knows how to handle his business. He will not yoke you up with an unbeliever. Desperation may cause you to walk by sight and make a decision you will regret later. This is why good sound marriage counseling is so important. Do not forsake counsel because you fear that you may hear something that may discourage you from getting what you think is a prize. It would be wise to know upfront that a person is not sent by God than to suffer in disobedience. God is the maker of marriages and everything God made was good. You have to work on relationships. They are not made in heaven, but can be heavenly if made by God.

God does not intend to give you a life that makes him unnecessary.

These two women of God, Mary and Martha were two unique sisters in the ministry. They were also Disciples of Christ. Jesus spent some precious time in the presence of these two sisters. When Lazarus, the brother of Martha and Mary had died, (St John 11) they sent for Jesus. When Jesus heard of this, he said, "This sickness is not unto death, but for the glory of God, that the Son of God might be glorified thereby." Jesus walked on toward Judea to answer the call of Martha and Mary. St. John 11:20(KJV) "Then Martha, as soon as she heard that Jesus was coming, went and met him: but Mary sat still in the house. Then said Martha unto Jesus, Lord if thou had been here, my brother had not died. "

Jesus went through a series of faith building to get the on lookers prepared for what he was about to do. St John 11: 35 (KJV) "Jesus wept." Where were the believers? Did Martha really believe? She possessed the same power, but did not have enough faith to exercise it. This grieved Jesus, so he stopped and cried. He knew he had much work to do. Many times, we spend time praying, fasting and sowing seeds, but we do not walk in expectation. Expectation requires preparation. If we are to believe that God will answer prayer and deliver on his promises, we must walk in earnest expectation. Expect nothing but God's best for your life.

In Luke 10:38-42(KJV) Jesus was found once again in the presence of two sisters, Martha and Mary. Martha welcomed Jesus into her house and had made much preparation for his visit. In verse 40, Martha brought it to Jesus' attention that Mary had left the kitchen and sat down at his feet and left her to work alone in the kitchen. (As if Jesus had not noticed) In verse 41, Jesus began to calm Martha's nerves, "Martha, Martha thou art careful and troubled about many things, v42- "But one thing is needful: and Mary hath chosen that good part, which shall not be taken away from her." In other words, nothing is more important when the word is going forth. The word brings revelation, the word brings light and the word brings life. Food is good and is needed to sustain life but bread alone cannot keep you sanctified.

Deuteronomy 8:3 (KJV) " And he humbled thee, and suffered thee to hunger, and fed thee with manna, which thou knewest not, neither did thy fathers know; that he might make thee know that man doth not live by bread only, but by every word that proceeded out of the mouth of the Lord doth man live."

Luke 4:4 (KJV) "And Jesus answered him, saying, it is written, that man shall not live by bread alone, but by every word of God." So sometimes you have to feast on the word and turn your natural plate over so God can give you what you are waiting for. We should seek the Lord for priority in our lives. Mary should you worship? Martha should you serve? The issue at hand is spiritual growth and maturity. There will be times Martha should serve, but at this time I will worship, said Mary. What are you doing when the word is going forth? Please take a moment to answer this question, because it will tell you what you really seek after. Mary needed time to take in spiritual food, for she knew that her natural food would always be there, but her spiritual food was getting ready to take flight and as Bishop Jones use to say after he had preached, "take all you can and please "can" all you can get. In other words, you are going to need this sister/brother. You need to get it while it is going forth. Sometimes stressing over small things sets you up for distractions that will cause you to miss God. The good part that Mary had chosen was the word, the bread of life, the everlasting father. The bread of life that will never allow you to go hungry, the living water that will never allow you to thirst again. Make the main thing the "main thing" and watch God move on your behalf.

It takes a special anointing to live the single life. It takes an anointing to live Saved, Sanctified and Single. Psalms 28:18- "Whoso walketh uprightly shall be saved: but he that is perverse in his ways shall fall at once." It is the Lord's desire that you live a life free from sin. Psalms 10:13- "For whosoever shall call upon the name of the Lord shall be saved." You will only attract what you are. If you hold up a standard and delight yourself in the Lord, he will give you the desires of your heart. The Lord wants to set you apart; he wants to make you whole. A whole person is complete in mind, body and spirit. Sanctification is a set up for God to move on your behalf.   St John 17:17 "Sanctify them through thy truth: thy word is truth." The Lord promises that he will keep you if you desire to be kept. St. John 17:12 "While I was with them in the world, I kept them in thy name; those that thou gave me I have kept and none of them is lost, but the son of perdition; that the scripture might be fulfilled."

To be single or married does not come without a price.

1st Corinthians 7:25-29 "Now concerning virgins I have no commandment of the Lord: yet I give my judgment, as one that hath obtained mercy of the Lord to be faithful. I suppose therefore that this is good for the present distress, I say, and that it is good for a man to be so. Are you bound unto a wife? Seek not to be loosed from a wife? Seek not a wife. But and if you marry, you have not sinned; and if a virgin marry, she has not sinned. Nevertheless, such shall have trouble in the flesh: but I spare you. But, this I say brother, the time is short: it remains that both they that have wives be as though they had none."

V32-34- "But I would have you without carefulness. He that is unmarried cares for the things that belong to the

Lord, how he may please the Lord. But he that is married cares for the things that are of the world, how he may please his wife. There is also a difference between a wife and a virgin. The unmarried woman cares for the things of the Lord that she may be holy both in body and in spirit: but she that is married cares for the things of the world, how she may please her husband."

V35-38- "And I this I speak for your own profit; not that I may cast a snare upon you, but for that which is comely, and that ye may attend upon the Lord without distraction. But if any man thinks that he behaves himself uncomely toward his virgin, if she passes the flower of her age, and need so require, let him do what he will, he sinneth not: let him marry. Nevertheless he that stands steadfast in his heart, having no necessity, but hath power over his own will, and hath so decreed in his heart that he will keep his virgin, does well. So then he that gives her in marriage does well, but he that gives her not in marriage does better.

While the devil wants you confused so that you will not seek God for a plan for your life, he never gives up trying to defeat you and cheat you out of your blessing. He comes to kill your faith in God, steal your testimony of waiting on God and destroy the destiny for your future family.

St. John 10:10 "The thief comes not, but for to steal, and to kill, and to destroy: I am come that they might have life, and that they might have it more abundantly." God is so good to us, he warns us of what the enemies' attacks are. If we do not take heed to the warnings, we are sure to be attacked head on. Knowing this, we must then accept the consequences of not waiting on God.

Seeking God for a mate will require great development. The key is not to look for that person that is right for you, but to be that person that is right. You can only give account for who you are. If you cannot prepare yourself for that special someone in God, how can you expect the other person to be what is right for you? Developing a consistent prayer and thought life will prepare your mind and spirit to be complete.

Psalms 63:11 says, "O God, thou art my God; early will I seek thee: my soul thirsts for thee, my flesh longs for thee in a dry and thirsty land, where no water is; To see thy power and thy glory, so as I have seen thee in the sanctuary." When you meet God early, it prepares your mind and spirit and balances your life to be a blessing to your future spouse. A relationship with God releases an authority and power like no other. God is able to do just what he said he will do. You just have to line up with his word and stay in his presence. Worshipping the true and living God, Jesus Christ puts you at an advantage over those with a self-seeking will.

John 4:24-"God is a spirit: and they that worship him must worship him in spirit and in truth." The spirit will guide you into all things and teach you those things you don't know about. The spirit brings revelation knowledge.

Galatians 5:16-17 "This I say then, Walk in the Spirit, and ye shall not fulfill the lust of the flesh. For the flesh lusts against the Spirit, and the Spirit against the flesh: and these are contrary the one to the other: so that you cannot do the things that ye would." V 25- If we live in the Spirit, let us also walk in the Spirit."

God wants you to completely depend on him to manifest his plan for you, minister to you and ultimately marry you. Your daily prayer should be, "Open the eyes of my heart Lord."

Ephesians 1:18-19 The eyes of your understanding being enlightened ; that you may know what is the hope of his calling, and what is the riches of the glory of his inheritance in the saints. And what is the exceeding greatness of his power to us-ward who believes, according to the working of his mighty power."

God wants to minister to you to show you his power to make your life great. Romans 10:17-"So then faith comes by hearing, and hearing by the word of God."

Romans 10:14-"How then shall they call on him in whom they have not believed? And how shall they believe in him of whom they have not heard? And how shall they hear without a preacher?

Hebrew 10:25-"Not forsaking the assembling of ourselves together, as the manner of some is; but exhorting one another: and so much the more, as you see the day approaching. With this being said, you must become affiliated with a Bible teaching church to build a good, strong foundation for your life.

God wants you in a Godly marriage; he will not yoke you with an unbeliever. Contrary to what some may believe. God is picky when it comes to your life. This is why he does not take kindly to your flesh dictating the destiny of your soul. Your soul depends on you yoking up with the right rib.

2nd Corinthians 6:14-"Be ye not unequally yoked together with unbelievers; for what fellowship hath righteousness with unrighteousness? And what communion hath light with darkness?

Plainly put, you have no business seeking a mate outside of the faith. Amos 3; 3-Can two walk together, except they be agreed? Again, I say that you will only attract what you are. It is imperative that you live so close to God that the person seeking or waiting will have to seek him to find you.

Every normal man desires a woman and every normal woman is waiting for a good man. Every leader desires followers. A leader who has no followers is on a lonely journey. The head/brain is the master over the body. Every prayer deserves to be followed with praise to God. If you live for God his love will be shed abroad in your heart. God will be your covering, stay close to him. It is his desire to give you good blessings. Every choice has a consequence, for every action there is a reaction. Seeking God brings positive results. If you are single and desire a mate. I advise you to be all that you can be in Christ. Seek to know who you are and whose you are. Some people put on acts to portray something or someone they are not only to marry and find out there is a dead cat on the line. The marriage starts to stink and the truth comes out. If you develop Godly character and integrity up front, truth and honesty prevails. Do not drag your old baggage into a new relationship. No one cares about how you were tricked by your ex- partner. Cast all your cares on God and leave them there. It is not fair to make a potential mate pay for what an old scum bag did. It is not even right to make a potential mate pay for what your parents did to you. Bag all that trash up, sit it by the road for waste management to dispose of it properly. Give your heart to God and all your unconditional love to your new mate and don't look back.

Luke 17:32 "Remember Lot's wife?

Genesis 19:26 "But his wife looked back from behind him, and she became a pillar of salt."

This can only signify one sure thing. Lot had her in front of him and he had her covered. She looked back from behind him and their future was instantly destroyed. This is what emotional, mental and physical baggage can do to a relationship. Let it go! Do not allow it to go forward with you. Your past does not belong in your future. Your past made you the pillar of strength you are today for a reason. God brought you to it, he allowed it and he brought you out to show you the newness of life in him. You must start a successful relationship with God as the head.

St. Matthew 9:16-17 "No man puts a piece of new cloth unto an old garment, for that which is put in to fill up takes from the garment and the rent is made worse. Neither do men put new wine into old bottles: else the bottles break and the new wine runs out, and the bottles perish: but they put new wine into new bottles and both are preserved."

Put your trust and hope in Jesus, who is able to make all things whole and new. Be strong in the Lord and in the power of his might. Bishop Clifton Jones use to preach. "Two weak saints do not need to hang together.' Likewise, two weak saints do not need to date or marry. One must be like the new wine skin or the new cloth and be able to endure until the other is strengthened. When Jesus was going about healing, he said on one occasion in St Matthew 9:28 and 29.

"Believe ye that I am able to do this?"

"According to your faith be it unto you."

Bank on those words of Christ and let him make you rich in his spirit and bless you with all good things that he provides for those who seek him first and love him. Be blessed in your desire to have a Godly mate and be that Godly mate whom Christ can bless someone with. Amen.

Finally

Although some things happen in our lives that make us who we are, they were never designed to define who we are destined to become. Looking back over my life, I have been writing in a journal for as long as I can remember. Now that I have lived and experienced some life lessons, I understand what a testimony is. But at the same time, I am at a time in my own life where I can see my true self emerging and waiting to erupt. I have truly learned to be content in whatever situation I may find myself in. Some lessons I have learned: You cannot share if you are not willing to give. You cannot laugh if you don't have a sense of humor and you cannot love unconditionally unless God has touched your life in such a way that you have a passion and compassion to give of yourself whole heartedly. Real love isn't love until you give it away. Love is action. Your mouth may be moving, but if actions are not displayed, you are just letting out hot air.

As you live you develop and your gifts start to emerge and if you are not in tune with your true self, you cannot identify who you have become. You may not understand why trials and test come your way, but know this, as you live for God, tests will surly come. Tests are not uncommon to man. 1st Peter 4:12-13 "Beloved, think it not strange concerning the fiery trial which is to try you, as some strange thing happened unto you: But rejoice, in as much as you are partakers in Christ's sufferings; that, when his glory shall be revealed, you may be glad also with exceeding joy." I was not mature enough to receive those words at one point in my life. The enemy was fighting me on every hand and I almost gave up. In my confusion, I befriended enemies who I thought were my friends. They didn't understand the plan God had for me. My testimony to you is that all good things come from God and if you hold on through your trial, in your darkest hour he will bring you over into the joy that awaits you in the morning. The joy of the Lord really is your strength. You have to praise your way through. I realized that if I had quit during the middle of my test, I would have failed God and myself. God entrusted me with much and believe me, much was required of me. Some people have been known to exit the testing procedure prematurely. Failing the test, only means that you will have to repeat it somewhere down the line. When it's your turn to be tested, if you are not properly prepared, you will fail. You must recognize that …

"For though we walk in the flesh, we do not war after the flesh: For the weapons of our warfare are not carnal, but mighty through God to the pulling down of strongholds; casting down imaginations and every high thing that exalts itself against the knowledge of God, and bringing into captivity every thought to the obedience of Christ. And having a readiness to revenge all disobedience, when you obedience is fulfilled." 2nd Corinthians 10: 3-6.

If you don't study the lessons that God puts before you, you will not recognize the enemy's tricks. The old system of flesh seeks to defend itself. It does not understand when to let go and let God work. When you come to yourself and realize that whatever you are holding on to in this carnal world is not your source of help, then and only then can you stand boldly in the face of the devil and declare that Jesus is the real source of all that is good. He will supply all that you need if you will fully surrender your life to him. He knows what you are hiding behind your back that belongs to the devil, but he wants you to freely surrender it or you can keep it, it's your choice. To live a life free of sin will take a commitment and dedication on your part. You will not begin to live a blessed life, complete with all these things that God has just for you until you live only for him.

Marriage is, and always will be the highest institution ever ordained by God. God never intended for marriage to be taken lightly and divorce never was an option from him. Marriage is a covenant not a contract. Marriage is one of the easiest promises to break. We sign leases that we are committed to. We sign for loans that we work like Hebrew slaves to pay back. We will work overtime to pay for things we cannot enjoy. We live a life to impress people who do not even like us. But who is fighting for marriages that honor God's word? People walk out of marriages everyday without second thoughts. It takes work to forgive, it takes work to stand in the face of trouble, and it takes work to stand when it looks dark. But Jesus gave it all on the cross because he was thinking of us. Marriage represents Christ and his Bride (the Church) in all aspects. You must make every effort to glorify God in your marriage. The world is looking for Godly examples. Sure we make mistakes, but we must not allow our mistakes to make us. God allows U-turns, but no detours in marriage. You may turn around and get it right, but you must not take what you think is an easier route.

I challenge you to step out of the flesh and walk in the spirit. Love without boundaries. Love unconditionally. Love completely. Love unselfishly. Give your all and I promise you, you will reap a harvest if you faint not. Is it easy? NO. Is it worth it? YES indeed. God is able to make your marriage all that it is meant to be. I am a witness and testimony to God's faithfulness to marriage and it is time for Christians to stand up and become representatives of God's goodness and mercy in marriage. Love, Love, Love and Love some more. "Love covers all sins. Proverbs 10:12. Love never fails and God is that Love. May God bless you in your marriage and give you strength to hold on through any situation. God is the master over every situation. Your marriage belongs to God, so honor him with it.

The 10 commandments of Marriage

1. Thou shall Love your mate more than you love your children, family or friends.

2. Thou shall honor the needs of your mate above your own needs.

3. Thou shall show your mate daily physical affection.

4. Thou shall pray daily for your mate.

5. Thou shall speak blessings into the life of your mate, therefore blessing yourself and your children.

6. Thou shall be honest with yourself and your mate.

7. Thou shall consult each other before making any decision that will directly affect your mate and family.

8. Thou shall keep the marriage bed alive and well.

9. Thou shall not cause any mental or physical stress to your mate.

10. Thou shall protect and provide for your mate at all times.